How to Get What You Want

A Short Primer for Ambitious People

By Jason Shen

Disclaimer: The author is not responsible for any harm that may come of a reader who attempts to act on the suggestions in this book. On the other hand, the author is willing to take full credit for any gains that come of a reader. Just kidding. Well, not really.

Version 1.2 // April 2016

Version 1.0 // Jan 2015

Table of Contents

Introduction

We all want things. And for the things that are in our control, we basically "get" what we want in the immediate term. But often, what we want in the very immediate term is not what we want later on.

We want to go out with our friends, but we're tired, and so we decide our immediate want is to order take out and go to bed early. Then Sunday rolls around and we wonder where the weekend went.

We want to ask that cute boy / girl out, but we decide that we our immediate want is to avoid the feeling of rejection by just being friends. Then we kick ourselves when they start dating one of our acquaintances.

I wrote this book[1] because I find the process of wanting things and then taking steps to fulfill that want to be fascinating. A

---

[1] I also wrote it because I thought it would be fun to do a two week holiday sprint between December 2014 and January 2015. I'd say both are valid reasons to do something =)

philosopher might call it setting ends and determining means. A psychologist might call it goal activation and enactment of goal-congruent behaviors.

Whatever the terms we use, I believe we could all think a little harder about the things we want, whether we've truly chosen to want them, and whether we're taking the most effective approach to get those things that we want.

This book doesn't have any simple answers or magic formulas. Nothing beats hard work, doing your own research, and experimentation. But this book might offer a new perspective, a few interesting case studies, and some research that might just help you get where you want to go, faster and more effectively.

You might have encountered some of the ideas in this book before. That's fine. My job is to help you put those ideas into practice. It doesn't matter how much you know — if you don't apply it, your knowledge isn't worth much at all.

Just by reading this introduction, you've already helped me get what I want, a new reader, so thank you. I hope your experience with this book helps you get what you want, too.

Best,

Jason Shen

Jan 2, 2015 — New York City

1. Starting Principles

Why this matters

Your agenda vs their agenda

On some level, this is a battle. A battle between you and the world.

I'm not saying the world is out to get you. The world is indifferent. But there are lots of other people out there who have plans, who have wants and who are happy to use you to achieve their aims.

One of the key reasons why its worth figuring out what you want, is because if you don't set the agenda, decide what you want and go after it, there are plenty of people who will make the decision for you.

It's fine if you don't know what you want, as long as you don't mind being a pawn.

The words we use

Why this isn't a book about chasing your dreams

Here are words we won't be using in this book:

- Desire. Too woo-woo.

- Need. Too melodramatic.

- Dream, wish or hope. Too soft.

- Objective. Too corporate.

It turns out the word *want* comes from old Norse word *vanta*, which means "to lack". If you want something, you feel like it's missing from you. To get what you want is to fill an empty space with something that belongs there.

In this book, I'll mostly be using the word "want" as a noun, and occasionally, "goal", to refer to the various things we are working towards.

We all want a lot of things and it's important to acknowledge the little ones ("I want to feel confident selecting wines when I go to a restaurant") as well as the big ones ("I want to start my own business someday").

The two types of problems

How it all boils down

Nearly every problem you'll ever encounter ultimately falls into one of two categories:

1) You don't know what you want

2) You don't know what steps to take to actually get what you want

In order to get what you want, you need to get a good handle on both what it is you want, and how to get it. We'll spend the rest of this book talking more about each.

The thing to keep in mind is that we tend to think our problem falls into the second category (the path, the how), but it is often the first category (the clear sense of purpose), that we're wrestling with.

When you get called 'selfish'

How to deal with guilt trippers

There are some who might consider the entire proposition of a book and a mindset oriented toward "getting what you want" to be bad. The words "selfish" or "self-centered" might come up.

But what kind of world ought we live in then? One where we do things we *don't* want to do? What would be the point of that?

No one said we couldn't *choose* to want things that are beneficial to others. In fact, as we will discuss later on, getting what you want is only possible when you give *other people* what they want.

If you don't live your life guided by your instincts, intuition, and rational thought, how would these critics suggest you direct yourself? By your parents? Your church? Your government?

Understanding what you want and going after it is perhaps the most human thing you or I can do. And hopefully we come to choose wants that are good for the world. But that is our decision, and it's one we have the right to make.

2. Understanding the Things You Want

Deciding what to want

It doesn't just happen

Wants appear to come out of nowhere, but the fact is, the things we think we want are often a product of the situation we're in, the stimulation in the environment around us, and the beliefs and worldview we hold.

When we walk past a window front during the holidays and we see that sweaters at Bloomingdale's are 35-50% off, all of a sudden we want to shop for sweaters. Is that a real want? Or is that something caused by our perception of the quality of brands sold at Bloomingdale's, a world view that getting a deal is a good thing, and the fact that buying gifts for the holidays is on our mind?

We have to invest time to select the wants we choose to pursue.

What do I want right now?

The guiding question

It seems so obvious but we often lose sight of what we really want, and get caught up in a routine, doing things we don't like and which serve no greater goal.

One weekend, I found myself in a bit of a rush. I had woken up late, and so didn't get to the gym till almost noon and I still had some errands to run, which meant I was going to be pretty late to a social event later that night across town. As I cursed myself for dragging my feet earlier that day, I remembered to stop and ask the question:

What do I want right now?

What I wanted was to enjoy my weekend. That's why I was going to the party. Rushing and getting there late wasn't going to be enjoyable. I didn't really know too many people at the party. So I decided to skip it, complete the errands at a relaxed pace, and have a quiet evening catching up on a book.

This is a small example of what it means to ask yourself the question "What do I want right now?" You'll find that there are many situations and examples where it becomes relevant.

What others want for you

Well-intentioned or not, they must be watched

It is easy to get confused about what you want when there are a lot of other people putting ideas into your head.

- Your mother wants you to move closer to home. But you love living in New York.

- Your coworker wants you to have one of the brownies she made for the office. But you're trying to cut back on processed carbs.

- Your friend wants you to go to that concert with her tonight. But you're working on side project tonight.

We all have social obligations. That's what makes us human.

We can want to have strong relationships with people we care about. But that doesn't mean we have to give in. There are usually different ways of fulfilling these wants while staying on track with the things you really want for yourself.

What we miss

Don't forget about opportunity costs

When we get obsessed with a big want, we sometimes miss out. We forget about what else we could want.

A number of my friends are attending or applying to business school. One of them is a user experience researcher and holds a degree from a top-tier school plus a Fulbright Fellowship.

Let's call her Sandi. Despite her strong academic credentials, Sandi is concerned that she might be limited later on in her career without a formal degree in business. She starts thinking about getting an MBA. She looks into the programs, attends information sessions, speaks to alumni, and decides she wants to go to business school. While it will be a lot of work, MBAs earn higher salaries and many senior executives at major corporations went to business school, so it seems like a good investment.

She's decided what she wants. Wonderful, right?

Maybe. The mistake that people make when considering a decision is that they often don't consider what they might miss out on. Getting an MBA will involve dozens of hours of work applying, two years in the program, and hundreds of thousands of dollars in loans to pay for tuition, plus the salary you could have been making had you kept working.

Sandi may not have considered the *opportunity cost* of going to business school. What else could she do with two years and $200,000+?

Sandi has to remember that her original want was to avoid getting stuck later in life, and her want is to accelerate her career and open up new pathways forward, and that getting an MBA is only one of many ways she can achieve that.

One way to never lose sight of the bigger want, is through asking 5 Whys, a process developed by engineers at Toyota to refine their manufacturing processes. Why get an MBA? (To get formal training about business) Why? (So that I have the credibility to talk about high level business issues) Why? (So that I can have a fulfilling career) etc.

When you're choosing the things you want to pursue, remember to consider what you're giving up in the process, and what else might be worth pursuing.

Training to resist the marshmallow

What you want now vs later

The study is now legend. A group of Stanford researchers in the late 60's found that about 30% of 4 and 5 year old children, were willing to sit in front of a single marshmallow and wait up to 20 minutes without eating it so they could get a second one.

These strong-willed kids grew up to score significantly higher on the SATs, and their teachers and parents were more likely to say they dealt well with stress, planned ahead, and stayed in control in frustrating situations.

But what does that mean for the rest of us? If we had eaten the marshmallow as a child, are we doomed to a life of mediocrity? Hardly. Willpower is a valuable asset, and it is one that we can build.

In one study[2], conducted in the mid 2000's, Australian researchers Megan Oaten and Ken Cheng, had participants start a 3x per week aerobic and anaerobic exercise regiment. Essentially, they had to exert willpower to go to the gym and workout when they were used to be sedentary.

---

[2] "Longitudinal gains in self-regulation from regular physical exercise." http://www.ncbi.nlm.nih.gov/pubmed/17032494

After a number of weeks, they were evaluated on an eye-tracking test that is used to measure willpower. Compared to a control group that didn't workout, the exercisers performed better. But more importantly, they also reported a variety of improvements, from doing more chores around the house, drinking less alcohol, going to bed earlier, and many other activities they often struggled to complete.

Oaten and Cheng have gone on to basically show that willpower can be trained, similar to a muscle, and it can become stronger over time — and apply to many areas of your life.

When dealing with what you want, you have to always think about timeframe. Often the things you want most (a fit body, a good GPA, the respect of your coworkers) involves skipping the short term want, the first marshmallow, in exchange for the long term one.

Train yourself to not eat the first marshmallow.

Don't let the present reality hold you back

What you want vs. what's possible

Sometimes we confuse what we can get with what we actually want. And while it's easy to get these mixed up, it's important not to.

In 1954, Roger Bannister set a world record, running one mile in 3:59.4. The 4 minute mile had become a white whale, with medical experts arguing that the human body wasn't capable of completing it. Prior to Bannister, the previous one mile record had stood at 4:01 for nine years. Less than a year later, someone else ran a sub 4 minute mile. Today, hundreds of American runners, and likely thousands around the world have achieved this feat.

Sometimes we can't even allow ourselves to want things because we don't think it's possible. Bannister was fast, but there was no reason why many of peers couldn't have broken the record either, since today, mere high school runners have broken the barrier.

When considering your Wants, don't let the present reality hold you back. Spend time with people you admire, who have done amazing things, and allow their achievements and can-do spirit to rub off on you, and allow you to want more.

More

We all want more

Since the dawn of humankind, we have wanted more. More fur, more meat, more land, more gold, more soldiers, more horsepower, more pixels. The human race would not have come to where we are today, a massive, sprawling group of interconnected organisms, if we had not constantly wanted more.

Those who say this is the work of capitalism are only a little right. Capitalism has allowed more people to believe they could indeed have more. As a peasant in a feudal society, you might want more grain, but you'd never dream of wanting four horses and a silver chariot. Today, we believe we can have more, and so we want more.

It's natural to want more. It's ok to want more. But there's a dark side too. The high-achieving student who doesn't know who she really is anymore. The billionaire who feels empty even as he closes another massive deal. It's because they lost sight of the deeper want. The want for recognition, for admiration, for intimacy, for excitement and the joy of the unknown.

My friend Lana once told me that a "lack of clarity about what you want cannot be replaced by simply wanting more of what you have."

Feel free to want more. Just make sure you're doing it for the right reasons.

How other people's wants affect yours

Peer pressure really works

We all know that teenagers are highly susceptible to peer pressure. That's why parents are often concerned when their children are hanging out with "the wrong crowd". But eventually we grow out of that phase, and learn to make decisions on our own right?

Not quite. Consider something as simple as purchasing a snack or a film on an airplane.

An assistant professor at the Stanford Graduate School of Business named Pedro Gardete recently looked at over 65 thousand transactions on nearly two thousand flights[3]. In findings he published in a working paper in fall of 2014, Gardete found that on average, people purchased just over 15% of the time when they were on a flight. But if someone next to them bought something, the chances that they would too grew by almost ⅓ — they then had close to 20% chance of buying.

Even in something so simple, seeing the person next to us order a beer or buy a movie, triggers a feeling within us to want to do it too. So we have to be careful about who we spend time with. Their wants will become ours.

---

[3] "Understanding Social Effects in the In-Flight Marketplace: Characterization and Managerial Implications" http://faculty-gsb.stanford.edu/gardete/documents/Social%20Effects-Oct-14.pdf

Why you need to Make a List

Sorting through your wants

Our heads filled with a lot of ideas about what we want, what we could want, and what we should want. That's normal.

The challenge is then how we deal with all that clutter. And the answer is so simple we might be tempted to skip it. But we shouldn't.

> *"Making lists is a great way to clarify thinking. You put down thoughts, order them, refine them, and even share them with others. ... The first thing I tell teams of people who are struggling is ML: Make a list."[4] - Scott Berkun*

Berkun is the author of five popular books on creativity, leadership, and innovation and has lead technology teams at Microsoft and Wordpress. His advice applies both to leaders of teams, and individuals looking to figure out what they really want.

So make a list. Preferably on paper and not on a digital device.

Think about paper as just an extension of your mind. You might brainstorm an issue without pulling out your laptop or phone. Jotting notes down on a piece of paper is just a way to have all

---

[4] The Year Without Pants: WordPress.com and the Future of Work
http://scottberkun.com/yearwithoutpants/

your thoughts down in one place. It's often too easy to switch tasks once you start typing.

If you're anything like me, once you get started, you'll find yourself surprised at how many things you want to do, have, learn, etc. Spend some time on it, mull it over, review it, and look at what bubbles to the top.

Skipping straight to the how without deeply considering the what is like speeding down the highway without any directions. You could be making great time, but you might not like where you end up.

What to do when we're unhappy

Where does it hurt?

When we're unhappy, we often believe it's because we aren't getting what we want. We decide then, that what we want are a bunch of things that we think will take the unhappiness away: throwing ourselves into work, heading to the bar, watching a lot of TV, heading on a long trip by ourselves.

Often, pursuing these wants just make us feel worse.

When we're deeply unhappy, the root of the problem is often that we really don't know what we really want. Spending some extra getting to the bottom of what actually upsets us, and what we really want is important. Because otherwise we'll waste a lot of time and effort chasing wants that aren't very meaningful.

3. Going After Your Wants

Do your homework

It's no longer about your grades, it's about your life

One of the most powerful ways of getting what you want is simply doing your homework. That means a few things:

- **Organize yourself.** If there's information or people to track, or multiple events or dates, put everything in a spreadsheet. Keep your calendar up to date. If you're not really familiar with the numbers, have them ready so you don't waste time trying to remember or look the figures up. When you are prepared, people are impressed, and you don't waste time looking for things. You look more competent.

- **Before a meeting - do your research.** What are you going to talk about? What message do you want to deliver? What's on their mind? What's going on in their world? Have they been in the news recently for something? What questions will they have? What are the next steps on timing?

- **Before a presentation, have all the context ready.** Know the three things you want people to walk away with. Arrive early. Know the most common objections you might hear, have responses to those objections ready.

Since so much of getting what you want involves convincing other people you know what you're doing, as well as using your time in the most efficient way possible, preparation is one your greatest assets. So few people actually make adequate preparations for things that you can look like (and act like) a major pro without a significant amount of effort.

Giving people what they want

It's not all about you

> *"You can get everything in life you want if you will just help enough other people get what they want."*

Zig Ziglar wrote those words back in 1984, but they are just as true today. We live in such an interconnected world that no matter what you might want, you're going to need the help and cooperation of other people to get there.

Doesn't matter if you want to conduct astrophysics research, learn to ride a motorcycle, be the opening act for Aziz Ansari, invent a new web development framework, or just try every rum bar in your city. It's going to be nearly impossible to fulfill your want on your own.

When we dig into our deeper wants, many of us find security and freedom to be core goals, which we try to fulfill with money and other tangible assets.

Well, what does it mean when someone pays you for something? They are engaging in *trade*. Whatever you have given them is worth more to them than the money they are giving you in return.

Even when someone donates to a cause like PETA, they are indicating that the knowledge that they've helped fight animal cruelty is more valuable to them than the $20 they've just given up.

So as you embark on your journey to pursue your wants, remember that the best and fastest way to get them is to give other people what *they* want.

To Plan or Not to Plan

That four-letter word

Plans.

Some people love them, others hate them. There are a couple ways to approach plans as you seek to get what you want.

- **Don't Plan.** Just go with the flow. Do what makes sense in the moment and constantly adjust your approach along the way. This works great for very open ended wants, like "Having a fun Saturday night bar hopping". Not planning can make it easier to just jump into action but the challenge is that you can get distracted and lose sight of your overall goal or get caught in a bad position because you didn't have what you needed. Even bar hopping requires thinking ahead enough to pick the right part of town, have enough cash on hand, and get some food in your stomach before you get started.

- **Make a traditional plan.** Figure out what milestones you need to hit, and starting where you are, make realistic estimates about how much progress you can to make with the resources you have, to figure out how to get to your goal. You can also list people or organization who can help you, along with reading and information that would be valuable alongside the tasks and schedule you set out.

- **Make a reverse plan.** As someone who didn't always like planning, I found this to be the way I came to appreciate planning. Set the date in the future when you'd like to get what you want. Maybe this is the day you want to start a new job. If that date is 3 months from now, what needs to happen before then?

  Well, you need to give two (or three, or whatever) weeks notice. You need to have signed a contract with a new company. You need to have interviewed multiple times with that company, and other companies. You need to have applied to work at those companies. You need to have written cover letters and sent an updated resume. All of these actions work you back to where you are now, putting the pressure on you to get it all done.

- **Just make a damn list.** Returning to the wisdom of Scott Berkun, even if you absolutely hate planning, simply making a list of tasks to accomplish, important dates, things that might help you, people you might want to reach out to, or anything else that you need to remember, is still better than not planning

The fact is, the world is an unpredictable place, and every plan starts becoming obsolete the moment you finish it. That can be really frustrating and cause you to lose faith in planning. But just because your plan changes (even a lot) doesn't make planning worthless. The real work is how the plan prepares you to tackle the problem.

Last thing I'll say about plans simply to quote General George S. Patton:

> *"A good plan, violently executed now, is better than a perfect plan next week."*

Sometimes you just have to power through

Taking massive action

At the end of the day, to get what you want, you have to get off your butt and do things.

The bigger the want, the more action you have to take. If you aren't getting what you want, there's a good chance *taking massive action*, a concept made famous by Tony Robbins, could help create results, build momentum, and move you closer to your goal.

It's hard to explain what it means to take massive action. It's much easier to tell a story.

Buford Taylor, an early engineer at Eventbrite, and the cofounder of an in-seat ordering app for venues, wrote about how someone he knew went from being a customer service rep at a pharmaceutical company with zero coding experience, to working full-time as a Quality Assurance (QA) engineer in 9 months[5]. He called her Jane.

---

[5] You are the average of your five closest friends http://bufordtaylor.com/you-are-the-average-of-your-five-closest-friends

Jane was unhappy in her job and noticed that her friends who worked as software engineers at Google actually seemed excited about their jobs, and felt that their work made a difference. It was like night and day. Moreover, one of these friends was also studying for their master's after work. When her frustrations hit a boiling point, Jane decided that enough was enough.

Some light inside Jane turned on around that time; she had a new mission. She would work in technology, and she would do it as a QA engineer. She sat down with her friends and they all helped determine the right path to get her where she wanted, if she was up to the challenge.

Keep in mind, this was late 2010. She had never written a single line of code in her life. She didn't know what a command line was. She had trouble understanding her smart phone.

One of her friends at Google was studying for his master's after work.

Jane followed suit and enrolled herself in the O'Reilly School of Technology for some crash courses on HTML/CSS/Javascript. Struggling every step of the way, she poured her after work hours into learning the way of front end development and basic web page manipulation. A few months into it, she was applying for a new job as a QA engineer.

Maybe it was bold determination or simple insanity that made her apply for roles she was incredibly under-qualified for, but she was thriving on the pain of failure. With every failed interview, she went home and studied every question that was asked to her, thoroughly ripped apart computer science topics that she never fathomed she would need to know. As she studied, she felt that all this hard work was making her lucky.

The first job she landed was nothing more than a $50 gig as a tester for an upcoming iPhone application. But she put it on her resume. She kept working at her goal and started learning Python while she applied for more jobs.

Jane eventually landed a full-time job at a 20-person startup as a QA tester.

It was an important milestone, but being a QA tester isn't the same as being an QA engineer. QA engineers don't just test products, they create programs that automate testing and ensure that the entire software development process as a whole is effective. Jane wanted to write code. So instead of taking a break and seeing where things went, she kept at it.

Ruby was the language of choice for QA automation in her company, so she took on the endeavor to learn Ruby and apply it to Watir (tool of choice). She started going to automation meetups for Selenium and Watir. Soon those meetups multiplied into women's Rubyist meetups, weekly study groups, and hackathons.

Six months later, she was confident that she was ready to execute her master plan. She applied for a company called PocketGems, and simply knocked them dead on the interview, but she didn't necessarily want to leave her startup for PocketGems. She just wanted to make a real difference.

With just a little guidance from her friends (she still needs to work on her negotiation skills), she leveraged the offer at PG to promote her to full QA Automation Engineer at her current company. She finally got what she wanted.

In 9 months, she went from never writing code in her life, to writing code every day. She tripled her salary. She has job satisfaction. The tools she solidifies helps change an industry for the better. Jane does things that matter.

You may have no interest in becoming a QA engineer. And that's absolutely fine. But I hope this story clearly illustrates what it means to take massive action, and the results that can come of it.

But what if you don't know anyone?

The hidden network around you

Sometimes, people use the excuse that they "don't have the connections" to get what they want. There is tremendous value in your network, even if you don't see yourself as a particularly connected individual. Often, we overlook the connections we have.

Legendary startup investor Paul Graham once wrote an essay about how being "relentlessly resourceful" was the key trait that he saw in great founders. Graham's article was shared widely across the web, and many people came to discuss its ideas on the social news sharing site, Hacker News. One commenter named nostramous wrote this:

> Yes, there are certain skills that make it easier to find information on your own. But this is also a function of the problem domain and how well you know it. If you give me a credit card and a problem statement, chances are that I can come up with a working webapp that solves the problem.
>
> But if you give me the name of a VC and tell me to go raise money – where do I start? How do I approach him? What will burn bridges and what won't?
>
> So my question to PG and any other resourceful folks out there is: how do you approach a problem domain in which you know

nothing, and manage to gain enough of a map of the territory so that you listen to someone's one-word suggestions and instantly grasp the implications?[6]

A few weeks later, I ran into Kevin Lackey, the co-founder of Parse, a mobile backend platform for mobile app developers that was acquired by Facebook for $85M in 2013. Lackey told me that he actually knew nostramous, because they were co-workers at Google back in the day and so he found the whole thing rather funny.

"I was thinking 'Dude, you know me. You know I've raised money with Parse. I would be happy to walk you through that stuff if you just asked.' "

If you had asked nostramous why he couldn't ask someone for advice on talking to a VC, he likely would have said that he "didn't have the connections". Yet, despite the rather helpless attitude he showed in the forums, nostramous actually had great connections to people who could help him with his challenge.

You might not have someone in your network who sold his company for 8 figures. But you might also be surprised. And more importantly, you are probably underestimating just how well connected you really are.

---

[6] "A Word to the Resourceful" https://news.ycombinator.com/item?id=3485933

How to ask for help

Technology is useful, but courage is essential

Let's say you want to try mining Bitcoin, because it'd be interesting and possibly lucrative. Assuming you've done your homework and you're looking to connect with like-minded people, how might you find them and ask for help?

- Post three sentence status update on Facebook: "Dear friends: I'm genuinely interested in getting more involved with Bitcoin. I've read the original Satoshi paper, looked into mining rigs like Y and Z, and dug around some of the Bitcoin forums. If you know anyone who'd be down to share a cup of coffee, a drink, or even do a phone call, I'd really appreciate it!" Watch the comments come out of the woodwork.

- Change your status on Gmail to something similar to what you have on Facebook.

- Find people talking about Bitcoin on Twitter. Start following them. Make sure you're tweeting Bitcoin related articles from time to time and have Bitcoin listed as an interest in your profile. Look for casual opportunities to tweet at them. Maybe they ask a question that you happen to know a lot about, or make a passing comment on TV show or coffee bar or piece of news that you can jump on. Eventually, you'll be able to ask them directly to connect.

- Look for a Meetup group or other type of event related to Bitcoin. Go. Don't try to meet everyone there. Instead, look for the friendly looking person who's also standing by themselves. Introduce yourself and ask them what they think is the thing everyone misunderstands about Bitcoin.

- Bring up your interest in Bitcoin in your everyday conversations. You don't have to get obsessive about it but dropping a comment here and there can lead to amazing serendipity

None of these steps are particularly difficult. But asking for help does put you out on a limb. So hopefully you're asking about something you really want. In any case, if you don't ask for help, you aren't allowed to pull a nostramous and complain that you "don't have any connections".

Asking the right questions

Learning from those who have come before you

As the old saying goes, most people learn from their own mistakes, but the wise learn from the mistakes of others.

To get what you want, whether it is starting a thriving bed-and-breakfast, waking up earlier, or getting over a bad breakup, you have to understand the shape of the challenge you have in front of you. The best way to do that through talking to people who have done it. Both successfully, and not.

We've talked about how to ask for help and create connections. Once you're talking to these people make sure you ask them these questions (along with anything else you want to know).

- **What made you decide to do this?** Understanding people's motivations are important because you will need to compare them to your own as you decide whether you really want this, or want it for the same reasons they do

- **What were your biggest surprises along the way?** This is a really important question because they probably had the same assumptions you do right now about how this experience is going to unfold, and their surprises indicate where those assumptions differed from reality.

- **If you could do it all over again, what would you change?** People don't like admitting their mistakes, so its often easier to ask them what they would do differently if they went back. Alternatively, you can ask them what they might do differently "next time".

- **What are the hardest parts about doing this?** You don't want to walk into anything with rose colored glasses. Make sure you know what you're up against as you decide to pursue that thing you want.

- **What are the best parts about doing this?** At the same time, you don't want to be scared off from what might be something great.

How do you know you're on track?

There's a reason why software has progress bars

It's important to find ways of measuring your progress and getting feedback on whether or not you're getting closer to your goal. Most of our goals are complex activities that make it difficult to determine whether we're on track.

So you have to build in ways of measuring progress. Whether that's proactively scheduling time for a work assessment from your manager each quarter, to keeping track of the number of steps you take, or even just counting hours we've spent working on our thesis — concrete feedback is crucial.

If things are going well, great. Full steam ahead. But if the feedback signals that you're slowing down or going in the wrong direction, that's when the check-ins show their true value. Because now you know you need to change course, and try something different, else you waste your time while moving further away from your goal.

There's another reasons to track your progress too. It'll make you feel better.

HBS Professor Teresa Amabile has been studying organizational psychology for 15 years, and she writes here in Harvard Business Review[7]:

> *"Of all the things that can boost emotions, motivation, and perceptions during a workday, the single most important is making progress in meaningful work. And the more frequently people experience that sense of progress, the more likely they are to be creatively productive in the long run."*

Here are some ways you can track progress with minimal overhead:

- Build it into your routine. If at the end of every day you do a quick update, or have a meeting every week where you review progress, it's easier to stick with it.

- Quantify things / reduce the options when necessary. Even for something as complex as mood, you could use a simple 1-3 range, or a set of emoji to represent how you feel rather than write an entire essay.

- Keep it visual and keep it in your face. During the startup accelerator Y Combinator, many founders bookmarked a website that listed the number of days till the big "Demo Day", and had that as their home page to remind them that time was limited.

Tracking your progress is important. Make sure you find a way that works for you.

---

[7] "The Power of Small Wins" https://hbr.org/2011/05/the-power-of-small-wins

Getting out of your own way

What has held you back in the past?

There have been times where you've screwed up in trying to get what you want. What were they?

There will be similar problems again in the future in this new thing (or set of things) you want. So how are you going to address it?

When you were on your last diet, maybe you agreed to go out with friends too often, and once you started drinking, you ended up getting late night burritos and blowing weeks of clean eating. So maybe this time you don't go out as often, or get friends to hang out at your apartment, or stay sober when you go out.

Too often people throw their hands up and say they can't do it. You have to be willing to step outside yourself, take stock of your strengths and limitations, and design a process that gets around your issues.

Remember, you are trying to get something you really want. Don't let anything, even yourself, stand in your way.

Inveniam viam

Latin for "go hard"

> *"Aut inveniam viam aut faciam" is Latin for "I shall either find a way or make one." The first word "aut" may be omitted, corresponding to omitting the English word "either" from the translation."*[8]

Supposedly this is what the great Hannibal told his generals when they protested that it would be impossible to cross the Alps by elephant. Whether or not it was a good idea to march animals adapted to tropical climates is one thing. The fact that he did it was another.

If you wanted a motto for tackling whatever is in front of you, you could do worse than "I will find a way, or I will make one."

---

8 Wikipedia http://en.wikipedia.org/wiki/Inveniam_viam

It's probably going to take longer

Sometimes you just need more time

Getting what you want isn't easy. Especially if you're a driven, ambitious person — because your goals tend to be bigger and you want to achieve them *now*. It's going to take time, effort, and resources.

In 2004, Bill Gates launched a special fund to invest in promising research projects run by "dream team" researchers in an effort to save lives and improve health outcomes in the developing world. After 10 years and $1B of investment, none of the projects are yet close to making any kind of major contribution.

Sure, these ideas were meant to be high-risk, high-return opportunities, but can you imagine being one of the wealthiest, smartest, best-connected people on the planet, and have little to show in the way of results after so many years and so much money?

Gates apparently used the word "humbled" four times in his update speech.

Whatever your want might be, it's probably not easy, or else you wouldn't be putting so much time, thinking, and effort towards pursuing it. You'd already have it by now.

But remember not to let yourself get into a "if only I had more …". If only you had more money, more staff, more connections, more exposure. Because the honest truth is, if you did, you'd be going after something bigger, and perhaps having to wait even longer to get it done.

Christopher Nolan had a treatment for the blockbuster movie "Inception" eight years before he was able to realize the vision. It took J.K. Rowling seven years to finish the first book of *Harry Potter*. Learn to embrace the long game even as you hustle each day.

No one is going to do it for you

You have to do it for yourself.

If you don't like your job, you can't wait for someone to just hire you out of the blue.

If you're not happy in your relationship, you can't expect your partner to just pick up on it and make it better. You have to talk it out and work through it, accept the compromise, or decide it's not worth it and walk away.

If you're not pleased with the way your body looks, it's not going to magically fix itself. You have to figure out a eating plan and workout strategy that will change it.

As children, we could sometimes wait for our parents or our teachers to fix a problem. At work, we don't always have to deal with an unpleasant or problematic element part of the company if it's mainly in some other department. But in our own life, we are now responsible.

If we don't like where things are going, we have to act to change it. Of course terrible things that aren't our fault can happen out of the blue. But most of the disappointments and unhappiness that we experience day-to-day are more in our control than we think.

And on the flip side, most good things in our lives happen because we worked to make them happen.

So let's make them happen.

4. What to Do When You Get Stuck

Practice Before You're Up

Don't wait until you're called

My friend Erica was a ballerina at the New York City Theater for 10 years. And for ballerinas, time is tracked according to how many Nutcrackers they've gone through.

There are different roles for children of each age. But Erica was always too tall for her age and couldn't do the younger roles, but wasn't experienced enough to do the older roles. Finally, when she was 16, she landed a small role, but it wasn't very challenging or exciting.

She'd sit in the back of the room, watching practice go by, not really paying attention. Then one day, her friend, who played a different, more interesting role, got injured in practice, and the headmaster immediately called Erica in to fill her spot. But because she wasn't ready, Erica faltered and couldn't play the part.

From then on, she was determined not to let that happen again. She stopped sitting, started practicing in the back of the room, making sure her instructors knew she was learning all the parts.

And sure enough, a few days before production, someone else got hurt. Erica got her chance to shine. And by proving herself there, she eventually earned better roles in the Nutcracker the year after.

Now at the New Yorker, Erica has twice been asked to step up and cover for a coworker when they were unavailable and she was the only one around to do the job. Because she had been carefully paying attention in meetings, looking at the attachments on the group emails was cc'ed on, and watching her coworkers, she was able to step up and do jobs that no one had ever formally trained her on, or asked her to do.

If you were her manager, wouldn't you be impressed? Where are there opportunities for you to practice now as you work towards the bigger wants you have in mind?

Sacrifices

How bad do you want it?

To get what you want, you have to give some things up.

- You can't both have a relaxing weekend, and run a bunch of errands and clean the apartment.

- You can't both sleep in and fit a workout in before you leave in the morning.

- You can't both go out with coworkers to happy hour and attend that workshop on advanced Javascript techniques

There are obviously exceptions and being creative about fulfilling different wants is important. But we often are unwilling to admit to ourselves what we are willing to give up to get what we want.

Tim Daggett was a member of the U.S. men's gymnastics gold medal team at the LA Olympics in 1984. He went on to start his own gymnastics training center where emblazoned on the wall were the words "how bad do you want it?"

To be an Olympic gymnast, to be a world-class anything, meant giving up a lot of fun things. Other sports, social events, dating, too much dessert, sleeping in on Saturdays, long vacations, etc.

So the question is: how bad do you want it? And what are you willing to give up to have it?

You can get almost anything you want, but it's pretty tough to have everything you want, all at once.

Want to Want

Getting meta

I remember having conversations with my cofounder Kalvin, who didn't like exercising, but knew it was important. He knew that he didn't want to exercise, but he wanted to want it.

This is a question that comes up in philosophy in the case of drug addicts. They crave the drug, but they also wish they were free of the craving.

While academics can debate what that means, a want to want situation calls for something simple: your goal should be to create (or eliminate) that want.

In creating a want, you often need to pair it with a different want. Like wanting to compete with yourself, or wanting to hang out with friends. If you don't like doing your math problems but you want to do well in your coursework, how can you make it a fun game? Can you find a study group and use that to drive your wants?

And if you want to no longer want something, you probably have to find some kind of a substitute. If you're hungry and want to stop snacking on junk food, can you try filling your pantry with fresh fruit. Or gulping a glass of ice water. Or going for a 10 min walk. Those activities might fulfill some of your wants (to stave boredom, to give your hands something to do) and dissipate the initial want (craving for salt, sugar and fat).

Ultimately, if you only "want to want" something, you're unlikely to follow through. So if it really matters to you, find something to attach your want to.

Dealing with Fear

The thing that goes bump in the night

Fears are a funny thing. It's important to take your fears seriously. Because our fears are often our biggest limitations. But sometimes what we fear is what we want most.

We want to start a company, to write a book, to change jobs, to ask her out, to get better sleep. But we are also afraid. We are afraid we will look stupid, we will miss out on other opportunities, we will be rejected, we will waste money, we will be laughed at.

There is almost nothing that I was actively afraid of (a final exam, a dark alleyway, a disappointed parent, an angry boss) which turned out to be worse in reality than in my imagination. I would guess the same might hold true for you.

This isn't to say terrible things don't happen. They definitely do. I've gone through some difficult experiences, but most of them were a bit of a surprise. Dislocating my knee on a vault landing. Having to fire someone. Getting pulled over. Wasting time and money on a project.

I'm not saying bad things are just in our heads. Bad things can and will happen. But they are most likely not the the things we're explicitly afraid of. Often our fears are just shadows in the dark - scary in our heads, but harmless when the lights come on.

Optimism is a force multiplier

The weapon you always want in your arsenal

In military parlance, force multiplication refers to an attribute or resource that, when utilized, allows a given force to be more impactful than without it. These might be things such as the element of surprise, better training, weather conditions, terrain, and technology.

General Colin Powell writes in his book on leadership this:

> *"Perpetual optimism is a force multiplier. The ripple effect of a leader's enthusiasm and optimism is awesome. So is the impact of cynicism and pessimism. ... Spare me the grim litany of the 'realist'; give me the unrealistic aspirations of the optimist any day."*

Optimism and pessimism appear to be at least somewhat ingrained traits, but they are also learned attitudes. Martin Seligman, the father of the Positive Psychology movement, has a process for training people to become optimists. It follows an ABCDE process:

- **Adversity.** Bad things happen to everyone. For instance, maybe you're a designer who didn't get assigned the project you were hoping for at your agency.

- **Belief.** That adverse event causes us to form a belief. For a pessimist, that might be "They didn't think I was good enough."

- **Consequence.** As a result of that belief, you start to experience consequences like questioning our previous work, getting less motivated to work on new projects, wondering if you're going to get fired.

- **Disputation.** The intervening step towards becoming an optimist is to dispute the belief that was formed. Perhaps you recall a conversation we had with our boss where she told us that you were doing such a good job on this current project, and that perhaps the company couldn't afford to remove you because you're so valuable. Maybe the client asked specifically for someone else.

- **Energization.** By casting doubt on our initial, negative beliefs, we remove the unpleasant feelings and consequences that come with the belief, causing us to hopefully feel more enthusiastic and energized.

If you feel you're a "natural" pessimist, consider exploring Seeligman's method[9] as a way to tap into the powerful force multiplier that is optimism.

---

[9] Learned Optimism: How to Overcome Life's Challenges http://brentonrussell.com/2010/12/06/learned-optimism-how-to-overcome-lifes-challenges/

5. Final Thoughts

Enough

What is that?

What is enough? That's a question each of us have to answer for ourselves. Steve Jobs, weeks before death, was still having meetings to discuss Apple related matters. What he wanted most was to produce incredible products that shape human lives on a massive scale.

Dipam Patel grew up in Houston, attended the University of Texas and earned an MBA. He had made a significant sum of money before he turned 26 years old, but soon came to wonder if this was all there was. He left for India, studied and trained for six years at a Hindu seminary, emerged as a monk named Gnanmunidas. Yet despite owning only a handful of possessions and literally not being allowed to touch money, he has no problem with material wealth.

As Arthur Brooks quotes him in a New York Times Op-Ed[10]:

> *"There is nothing wrong with money, dude. The problem in life is attachment to money." The formula for a good life, he explained, is simple: abundance without attachment."*

It's hard to know what enough is. A bowl, two robes, and prayer beads is enough for Swarmi Gnanmunidas. It's probably more for the rest of us, which is fine. But it's something we have to wrestle with if we hope to be satisfied as we continue pursuing our wants.

---

[10] Abundance Without Attachment http://www.nytimes.com/2014/12/14/opinion/sunday/arthur-c-brooks-abundance-without-attachment.html

Failure

How to deal with the F-word

Sometimes, despite your best efforts, you don't get what you want. And that can suck, no question.

I ran my first marathon in 2012. I thought I had trained well for it, but I sort of missed a crucial training window and didn't get some of the really long runs in. On race day, I went out too fast, ran out of steam, and ran a 4:50 time. I wasn't happy about it and vowed revenge.

Two years later, I had my chance. I got a charity bid for the 2014 NYC marathon, and trained hard all summer. I got some great long runs in, including an 18 miler in the rain, and 20 miles over a weekend. I felt ready.

Then race day came, and the weather was low 40's with a ton of wind. After training all summer and being a bit rushed going into the last week of the race, I didn't have enough layers during the race, and really struggled with the cold. After 4.5 hours, I had finished 20 miles but was basically walking and shivering like crazy. I knew those 6 miles were going to take another 2 hours, and I was going to get pneumonia. Part of me wanted to be stubborn, bite the bullet, and just plow through. But I was going on an international trip 3 days later and I knew I couldn't risk it.

I was frustrated. After months of training, I didn't beat my previous time. I didn't even finish the damn race. Total failure.

But I appreciated just how humbling that experience was. Going into something that you thought you had a handle on, and realizing that "Oh shit, I do *not* have a handle on this" is an amazing experience. It is not something we get to experience every day, and for that I'm grateful. And I'm also grateful for the fact that when I finally do run a marathon time I'm happy with, the story is going to be *that* much better.

Playing in your comfort zone is lame. If you get everything you want, when you want it, on the first try, you are clearly thinking way too small.

Failure isn't final. Failure is an opportunity to learn some really important lessons about the world and yourself. For instance, I'll never underinvest in race day prep, ever again. Perhaps after falling short of your sales quota by 50%, you'll adjust your target for next month. Tweak, fix, and iterate.

Scott Adams, the creator of *Dilbert*, has a very particular view on how he treats failure. Here he's commenting on the oft-quoted Nichetze line: "What doesn't kill me makes me stronger":

> *Becoming stronger is obviously a good thing, but it's only barely optimistic. I do want my failures to make me stronger, of course, but I also want to become smarter, more talented, better networked, healthier and more energized. If I find a cow turd on my front steps, I'm not satisfied knowing that I'll be mentally prepared to find some future cow turd. I want to shovel that turd onto my garden and hope the cow returns every week so I never*

have to buy fertilizer again. Failure is a resource that can be managed.[11]

That's a pretty good way to look at it.

---

[11] "Scott Adams' Secret of Success: Failure" http://www.wsj.com/articles/SB10001424052702304626104579121813075903866

Can you be too ambitious?

What happens when you bite off more than you can chew?

Most of us could dream bigger than we do today. Maybe we should try to complete our 5 year plan in just 3. Maybe we could expand our recycling program to encompass not just our school but the entire district, the entire state.

There does exist however a very small minority of people for where encouraging them to dream bigger is actually a bad idea.

I was once a member of the board of directors for a nonprofit organization that ran entrepreneurial competitions at college campuses. In reviewing the plan for next year, I saw the executive director had planned run 100 competitions, an ambitious target that was twice the target from the year before. Growing by 100% as a small organization isn't unheard of, but when our goal last year was 50 and we had barely hit 24, it was foolish to aim for 100.

If you're someone who routinely sets huge goals and falls short constantly. If you are constantly disappointed by your own performance, the answer isn't to set your sights lower, but to adjust your approach and lengthen your timeline.

Recognize that you aren't getting what you want, and not only that, but you're making it more difficult for yourself to get what you want in the future, because you're causing yourself and others to lose confidence in your abilities.

Focus on creating smaller wins. Start building momentum. If you've been trying to land a six-figure job for six months and you're still unemployed, start by taking something part-time, or doing some consulting work. See if you can develop new skills or expertise in something valuable. Apply for different jobs or in a different industry.

It's fine to still aim for the high-paying job, but like Gates, you'll have to allow yourself to be humbled by the magnitude of your challenge. Don't give up. Press on and play the long game.

Prepare to change

Getting what you want makes you a different person

We often don't like change. But change is inevitable when you're trying to get what you want.

It's a simple rule of thumb that the bigger the thing you want, the more you'll have to change to get it.

- Saving up for a vacation - small changes in spending

- Changing jobs - bigger change in your lifestyle

- Changing industries - even bigger change in who you interact with and what you do

We are shaped by every experience we have and every want we identify and pursue. Hopefully that thought doesn't scare you, but instead, leaves you excited and hopeful for the person you will become.

Conclusion

As human beings, we are driven by our wants. Our entire civilization is built around fulfilling our wants. Our want for shelter, for warm, for entertainment, for fast travel, for a feeling of community and contribution, for recognition and reward.

And yet so often, we seem to work towards wants that don't really satisfy us. Or we know what we want, but feel helpless to actually accomplish it.

That's what this book is all about. It's about asking good questions, making lists, and not getting swayed by the crowd. It's about doing your homework, developing plans, giving others what they want, and getting out of your own way.

I hope you enjoyed this book and found it useful. I'd love to hear from you if you have thoughts on the book. Reach me at @jasonshen on Twitter or jason@jasonshen.com

For more articles and ideas like the ones found in this book, visit me at my blog, *The Art of Ass-Kicking*, at http://jasonshen.com

About Jason Shen

Jason Shen is a Product Manager at Etsy, a global marketplace for unique and handmade goods, and writes about business, technology, and culture on his blog, *The Art of Ass-Kicking*.

He previously cofounded a venture-backed transportation startup, served as a Presidential Innovation Fellow, and set the Guinness World Record for Aztec Pushups. His work has appeared in *The New York Times*, *Wall Street Journal*, *Vanity Fair*, and the *San Francisco Chronicle*.

Jason earned a B.S. & M.S. from Stanford University, where he was captain of the Stanford Men's Gymnastics championship-winning team. He holds the Guinness World Record for the most Aztec pushups completed in one minute.

"He especially enjoys computer work, games and making things. Jason has a wonderful curiosity and wants to explore everything ... because of his activity level he is an exhausting child to work with."

— Ellen Ward, Jason's Kindergarten teacher.